Amelia's Flying Machine

Amelia's Flying Machine

BARBARA SHOOK HAZEN

Illustrated by Charles Robinson

ESEA Title IV

Doubleday & Company, Inc., Garden City, New York

For Melissa and Deralyn,

who will undoubtedly do all sorts

of exciting things—

and for Lisa, who already has.

LIBRARY OF CONGRESS CATALOG CARD NUMBER 76–51861
ISBN 0-385-07945-1 Trade
       0-385-08139-1 Prebound

text copyright © 1977 by Barbara Shook Hazen
illustrations copyright © 1977 by Charles Robinson

Stuck at Home

"But why can't I go with you?" asked Amelia. It was the summer of 1905, the hottest one ever recorded in Kansas. Amelia and her father sat on the front porch of the farmhouse, drinking glasses of ice-cold lemonade.

Amelia gave the porch swing an extra hard push. "I want to go with you so much," she said. "I love trains. Besides, you said that travel was good for me—that a girl my age should go new places and meet new people."

"I know, I know," sighed Amelia's father. "And I meant it, Meeley. But this time is different. I have to do some work for the railroad. And your mother has to help me hunt for a new house."

Amelia's father puffed on his pipe. "Besides,

Grandma Otis will need your help when your cousins Katherine and Lucy come for a visit. Someone has to stay and show them a good time."

He spoke gently. "Try to understand, Amelia, Grandma is getting a little too old to chase after four lively girls."

"Grandma Otis isn't too old," Ameilia protested. "It's just that we can run faster than she can!"

Amelia's father knew how disappointed she was.

"Tell you what," he said. "If you stay out of mischief and I get a good report from Grandma, I'll take you on my next trip, to Chicago."

"To Chicago!" Amelia clapped her hands excitedly. "To the World's Fair! Could I ride on the rolly coaster, like Jimmy did, and everything?"

"And everything," Amelia's father said, smiling. "That's a promise." He paused. "As long as you don't give Grandma a hard time."

"Oh, I won't," said Amelia. "I'll do everything Grandma says. I know all her rules by heart."

She counted them off on her fingers. "Act like a little lady all the time. Don't try to do every fool thing

Jimmy does. No football in the parlor. No rat traps in the pantry. No riding bareback or swimming in the river. And wear a dress and stockings—even if they itch." Amelia made a face.

In a voice that sounded like Grandma Otis, she said, "My dear Amelia Mary, do you mean to tell me that your mother *made* those trousers you are wearing? And your father gave you a football for Christmas? Mercy me! In my day little ladies were content to roll their hoops and dress their dolls."

"Well, the world is changing," Amelia's father chuckled. "And perhaps it's changing a little too fast for Grandma. Why just the other day I heard about two brothers named Wright. They built a flying machine. It had wings, and it flew like a bird. And they flew *in* it. Imagine that!"

Amelia laughed. "Oh, I can!" she cried. "I'd like to fly, too!"

Her father smiled. "Maybe you will someday. But now, young lady, it's time for bed."

What To Do

Amelia got up early the next morning to say good-bye to her mother and father. She felt a sharp pang of disappointment as she watched their carriage roll down the road.

"'Bye, Meeley," her father called as he waved. "Be good."

"'Bye!" Amelia waved back.

Then she walked down the road to the Watson's pasture and patted the horse through the fence. Amelia liked animals, especially horses.

"I'm going to Chicago soon," she told the horse. "Oh dear, why does 'soon' always seem so far away. I want to go *now!*"

When she got back to the farmhouse, her cousins had arrived. Katherine and Lucy were sitting in the hammock. Amelia's little sister, Muriel, was sprawled out on the grass.

Katherine, her older cousin, fanned herself. "Wow, it's hot," she said. "What can we do on such a hot day?"

"I'd like to go swimming," said Lucy. "Remember when we made a raft and took it down the river?"

"We can't," said Amelia. "That's one of Grandma's new rules. No more swimming in the river. Only in the pond. And I've got to get a good report from Grandma or Father won't take me to Chicago with him."

Lucy groaned. "The pond's no fun. It's not even over your head."

"What *can* we do?" Muriel asked.

Amelia looked up at the blue sky. A big bird was circling above the barn.

"I'd like to fly like that bird."

Katherine smoothed her skirt. "That's silly," she sniffed. "People can't fly. Only birds can fly."

"Katherine's right," agreed Lucy. "People can't fly. They'd fall."

"People can so fly," said Amelia. "My father told me all about it. He said two men built a flying machine that had wings like a bird. And they flew in it!" She began to flap her arms, and whirled around and round on the front lawn.

Just then Jimmy Watson rode by. He lived on the farm next door. He was about Amelia's age.

"Hey, Amelia, you're some bird!" Jimmy called. Then he whistled through his teeth.

He rode closer. "Want to see what I can do? I can ride no hands. Bet you can't do that, Amelia!"

Jimmy turned and headed his bike back down the drive. Halfway down, he took both hands off the handle bars. "See?" he yelled.

"I bet I can!" cried Amelia. She ran after Jimmy.
"Let me have a turn."

"Okay, try," said Jimmy. He got off the bike and
Amelia got on. She turned around and started back up
the driveway. She took one hand off the handle bars.
Then she took the other hand off.

"See, smartie," she called. "I can ride no hands, too."

Just as she said it, the bicycle hit a loose stone. The front wheel spun and the bike skidded. Amelia flew into the air and fell on the grass.

"Well, look at that," laughed Jimmy. "Amelia really can fly. She doesn't even need wings!"

Amelia pulled herself up and made a fist at Jimmy. "You think you're so smart," she said. "Well, you're not. You're just a big show-off, always bragging about all the dumb things you do. Let me tell you," she said, "I can do anything you can!"

"Seeing is believing," Jimmy taunted.

Amelia sprang to her feet.

"And I'm going to ride on a rolly coaster, too," she said, "when my father takes *me* to the Fair!"

"The rolly coaster? Boy, that's something I'd really like to see." Jimmy laughed. He got back on his bike and rode away.

Amelia's Bright Idea

"You sure were bragging yourself that time," said
Katherine after Jimmy left.

"I know," said Amelia. "But I really am going to
the Fair. Honest. Father said he'd take me—*if* I don't get
into any mischief while he's gone."

"You're not in any yet," said Lucy. "We're not
doing anything. I'm bored. Can't you think of something
we could do, Amelia?"

"Come on, Meeley," urged Muriel, chiming in.

"Hmmmmm," said Amelia. She sat cross-legged on the grass and looked straight ahead.

"What are you staring at?" asked Lucy.

For several minutes Amelia didn't answer. She was deep in thought.

All at once she snapped her fingers and sprang to her feet. "I've got it!" she said.

"Got what?" asked the others.

"What we'll do today," said Amelia, smiling.

"What we'll do is build a rolly coaster. Then we can all have a ride—and show Jimmy Watson a thing or two."

"You're kidding!" said Katherine, doubtfully.

"I am not!" said Amelia.

"How can we?" asked Katherine. "None of us has ever even seen a rolly coaster."

"I've seen pictures," said Amelia. "I'll think of a way."

Amelia pointed toward the barn. "See that big pile of boards," she said. "We'll use those for the track."

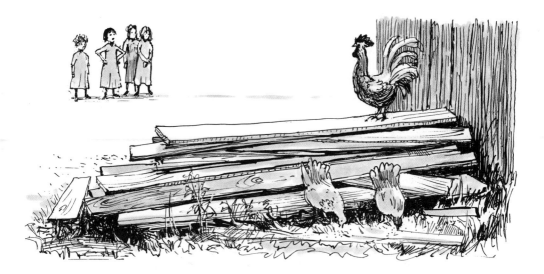

"What will Grandma say?" asked Muriel with a frown.

Amelia tossed her head. "Grandma doesn't have any rules about *not* building a rolly coaster," she said. "At least not yet!"

Amelia beckoned to the others. "Follow me. To the barn. To our rolly coaster."

When they got to the pile of boards, Amelia said, "What we'll do first is look for boards the same size. We'll nail the wide ones together to make the track bottom. Then we'll nail narrower ones on each side to make a rim, so the car doesn't fall off the track."

"What car?" asked Katherine doubtfully.

"That's easy," said Amelia with a grin. She pointed to another pile of old boxes and discarded household fixtures. "That's Grandma's junk pile," she said. "Grandma saves everything, including old orange crates. We'll take the best one and use it for the car. It will be a tight fit, but it will do."

"It sounds nutty to me," said Katherine, shaking her head.

"Not to me," said Muriel. She jumped up and down excitedly. "I think it sounds like fun. I want to if Meeley wants to."

"You always do," sighed Katherine.

The girls went right to work. They lugged the
longest boards onto the ground. Then they matched ones
that were the same length and laid them side by side.

Then they started hammering. They hammered all
the long hot morning and into the afternoon.

"Whew, I'm boiling," said Katherine as she laid down the last board.

"Me, too," said Lucy, wiping her face. "All I want to do is go swimming—anywhere—even in the pond. I've never been so hot."

"It's really a scorcher," admitted Amelia.

"Meeley, can we?" asked Muriel hopefully.

"Not yet," said Amelia. "The track's just about done. But the car isn't. We still have to put wheels on the orange crate."

"What wheels?" asked Katherine. "I doubt if Grandma saves those." She nodded toward the junk heap.

"Not there," Amelia said cheerfully. "Follow me." She headed for the barn.

Inside, Amelia pointed at one of the barn walls. "What do you see?" she asked.

"Just rusty old roller skates," said Katherine.

"Me, too," said Lucy and Muriel.

"That's not what I see," said Amelia. "I see rolly coaster wheels."

Amelia took the skates off their hook on the wall. She spun one of the wheels. "What we'll do is take the wheels off the skates," she said. "Then we'll clean them up and put them on the bottom of our rolly coaster car."

"I just hope it goes fast," groaned Katherine. "My hand hurts, and I'm tired of hammering."

"It won't take long," promised Amelia. And it didn't. The girls took the wheels off the roller skates with pliers. Then they got some heavy nails and hammered them through the center of the wheels onto the front and back ends of the orange crate.

Amelia gave the last nail an extra hard whack. "Done!" she said, putting her hammer down.

"It's about time," said Katherine, wearily.

"Last one in is a slow poke," said Lucy. She raced ahead to be the first in the water. Katherine took off after her.

"Wait!" called Amelia. "Help me put the track up into the barn window. I want to make sure it works."

There was no answer. Katherine and Lucy were already on the other side of the barn, halfway to the pond.

Amelia looked down at her own sweaty hands and dusty stockings. "I guess we have done enough for one day," she said to Muriel. "Besides, Grandma will have a conniption fit if we aren't cleaned up by supper. Let's go."

"Goody!" said Muriel. She ran ahead down the path toward the pond.

The girls jumped in with their clothes on. The pond wasn't very big and the water wasn't very deep. But it felt cool and good.

Afterward, everyone lay on the grass and spread out their skirts to dry.

"Wow, that was a lot of work for a hot day," said Lucy, looking at a blister on her hand.

"It sure was," agreed Amelia. "But it was worth it."

"Hmmmm," said the others, too tired to talk much.

Trial Run

The next day Jimmy came back on his bicycle. He rode by the barn just as the girls were setting up the roller coaster.

"Not bad," said Jimmy when he saw it. "Not bad at all, for girls."

"What does that mean?" asked Amelia, tossing her head.

"Nothing much," said Jimmy. Then he asked, "Does it work? That's what I want to see."

"You will," said Amelia. "Just wait."

Jimmy leaned his bike against a tree. He sat down on the grass and watched. "Who's going to go first?" he asked.

Amelia scooped up some pieces of straw. She broke off three short bits and one long one.

Then she turned to the others. "We could draw straws. That would be fairest."

"No thanks," said Katherine. "Not me. You go first, Amelia."

"Yes, you first," said Lucy. "It was all your idea."

Muriel looked up at the track slanting out of the hayloft window and shuddered. "Not me, Meeley," she said. "It looks awfully high."

"See," said Jimmy smugly. "Your sister is scared. Your cousins are scared of things like rolly coasters." Girls are always scared of things like rolly coasters."

Amelia faced Jimmy squarely. "Is that so?" she said. "Well, I'm a girl, and I'm not scared. I'll gladly go first!"

Amelia tested the track to make sure it was firmly set on the ground. Then she picked up the roller coaster car and carried it into the barn.

She carried it up the ladder to the hayloft and placed it on the wooden track. And then she squeezed herself inside the car. It *was* a tight fit.

She pushed herself part way out the barn window.
She held on tight to the track sides and looked out. It
was a long way down.

"What are you waiting for?" Jimmy called. "Are you scared?"

"Nope, not a bit!" said Amelia, letting go of the track sides.

The orange-crate car started to roll. It went faster and faster down the track.

Amelia hugged her knees and held on tight. "Whee!" she cried. "I'm flying!"

The car gathered speed as it raced down the track and hit the ground with a hard bump.

It landed so hard that it flipped over. Amelia flew out and fell on the ground. She lay on her stomach moaning, "Oooooooooooh!"

Katherine and Lucy and Muriel raced to her.

"I told you so," scolded Katherine. "You should have listened, but you never do."

"Are you hurt?" asked Lucy, trying to see Amelia's face.

Muriel just sobbed, "Oh, Meeley!"

Even Jimmy looked worried. He held out a hand to help Amelia up. "Are you okay?" he asked hesitantly.

"Sure. I'm okay," Amelia gasped. She turned herself over and brushed the dirt off her dress.

Then she sat up and folded her arms. Her expression was stubborn. "I'm okay, all right," she said. "But the track isn't. I made a stupid mistake."

Amelia paused. Then she frowned. "What's wrong is that the track is too short," she said. "That makes the slant too steep. And that's why the car hit the ground so hard.

"What we have to do," she said, getting up, "is add more boards and make the track longer."

"Why don't you just call it quits, huh?" suggested Jimmy.

"Not now!" said Amelia. "Not when I know what went wrong." She looked at Jimmy, "Come back this afternoon. You'll see how well it works."

Jimmy walked toward his bike. "You sure are one nutty girl," he muttered.

Back to Work

"Back to work," said Amelia as Jimmy biked out of sight.

"Not me," said Katherine. "My hand still hurts from yesterday. Besides I'm sick and tired of doing what you want to do all the time. I quit."

Katherine headed toward the house.

"Wait for me," called Lucy. "I'm coming with you."

Muriel hung back. "I'll stay," she said. "I'll help."

"Thanks, Murry," said Amelia, giving her a hug and a hammer.

Soon they were at it again. Amelia and Muriel laid the track on the ground. They added more boards until it was twice as long as before.

It was hard work, and it seemed even hotter than the day before. Both girls felt wilted and weary.

Amelia ripped her stockings and Muriel got a splinter in her little finger. "Just a little longer," Amelia kept saying. "Just a few more boards."

They were almost done when Katherine and Lucy
came back down the path. They were carrying
something.

"Lemonade, anyone?" asked Katherine.

Then she said, "I'm sorry, 'Melia. I didn't mean to get mad. It's just that you're so bossy sometimes. And I didn't tell Grandma."

"I'm sorry, too," said Lucy. "Do you still need help?"

"Just more lemonade," Amelia gulped. "And just in time."

When the lemonade was gone, the girls all helped
set up the track.

"It looks okay," said Amelia, standing back. "Let's
just hope it works this time."

"And hope Grandma Otis doesn't spoil everything," added Lucy. "She said she was going to take a nap. She sounded suspicious. She wanted to know what we were up to and why I had so many scratches."

"What did you tell her?" asked Amelia.

"The truth, of course," smiled Lucy. "I told her we were making lemonade and were going to take it out to you. Then I asked her if she wanted some."

"Then Grandma looked down her glasses and said, 'Young lady, I smell something fishy.' And I said, 'But, Grandma Otis, we haven't been near the river.'"

"And then we got out of there fast," said Katherine. She shook her head, "If Grandma decides to come out here, you're a goner."

"At least my trip to Chicago is," said Amelia.

Muriel's eyes grew big. "What are you going to do, Meeley?"

"Hope Jimmy comes over soon and hope Grandma takes that nap," said Amelia crossing her fingers.

It Works!

Jimmy came over soon. "I wouldn't miss this for anything," he said with a grin.

Amelia made a face at him. Then she turned to the others. Once more she asked, "Shall we draw straws to see who goes first?"

"Not me," said Katherine. "Not after last time."

"Don't look at me," said Lucy.

Muriel shook her head. "Not me, Meeley," she said. "But if you go, I'll keep my fingers crossed."

"See," said Jimmy. "Didn't I tell you so! Your cousins and your sister are scared silly, and I'll bet you are, too. Only you're too stubborn to admit it. Girls are scaredy cats."

Amelia stamped her foot. "That's not so," she said. "I'm not scared. Just you watch."

Once again she carried the orange crate up the ladder to the hayloft and climbed into the car. Then she pushed herself halfway out of the hayloft window.

There she paused and took a deep breath. "It's got
to work," she whispered to herself. "It's just got to."

"What are you waiting for?" teased Jimmy. "Santa
Claus? Or me to try it for you?"

Amelia glared at Jimmy.

"Don't listen to him," yelled Lucy.

"Don't do it," said Katherine under her breath.

Muriel turned her head. She crossed as many fingers as she could. She closed her eyes tight. She didn't want to watch.

But she did want to see what was going on. When she opened her eyes to peek, she looked up and screamed, "Stop, Meeley! You can't go!"

The warning came too late. Amelia had just let go.
The car started to roll. As it picked up speed, it
went faster and faster down the long track.

Amelia felt the speed and the slap of wind in her face. "Wow! Look at me," she cried out. "I'm really flying!"

The orange crate kept going. It rolled to the end of the track, and then onto the ground. Amelia waved and grinned at Jimmy as she went by, and he grinned back at her.

The car finally came to a stop—right by a pair of black-stockinged feet.

"Oh-oh," gulped Amelia, looking up.

Grandmother Otis stared down at Amelia. Her hands were on her hips. Her eyebrows met in a disapproving V.

She spoke in her slow we'll-get-to-the-bottom-of-this voice. "Amelia Mary, what are you up to? And what kind of fool contraption is this? I suspected something. And I suspect your father will have something to say when he hears about it."

Grandmother Otis tapped her foot. "Young lady, was all this your idea?" she asked. "Or did somebody put you up to it?"

Amelia groaned. Telling the truth meant missing Chicago and the Fair and going with her father and everything.

"Yes, Gram," she said in a small voice. "It was all my idea." Then she sighed deeply.

Grandma Otis sighed, too. "Amelia Mary, I daresay I don't know whatever will become of you if you don't . . ."

"Ma'am," Jimmy interrupted, "it really wasn't Amelia's fault. I mean, she made it and rode on it, but I guess I kind of put her up to it."

Grandmother Otis turned toward Jimmy. She

squinted through her glasses. "I might have thought so," she said. "I didn't think any granddaughter of mine could do such a foolhardy thing."

She shook her finger at Jimmy. "Yes, I should have known you were behind this, Jimmy Watson. You have a habit of getting my girls in mischief. Why, I have half a mind . . ."

Amelia bolted to her feet. "But, but, Grandma. Jimmy's not to blame. I'm the one who . . ."

"I don't want to listen," said Grandma Otis sternly.

She picked up her skirts. "Amelia, Muriel. Girls. Come with me," she ordered.

"As for you, young man," she squinted hard at Jimmy, "You stay right here and take down this contraption. Right now. Break it up, every bit of it, mind you."

She turned on her heels and headed for the house.

Amelia hung back. "It isn't fair," she said to Jimmy. "You're getting the blame. It *was* my idea."

"So what!" Jimmy shrugged. "She'll get over it, and you'll get to go to Chicago. She never tells my pa, and she won't tell yours either."

"Know something," Amelia smiled. "You're really okay, for a boy."

Jimmy grinned back. "Just send me a postcard with something nutty on it like, 'Girls can, too!'"

"That's not so nutty," said Amelia. "Someday, Jimmy Watson, you'll see what a nutty girl can do. Just you wait."

Then she stuck out her tongue and skipped off after the others.